DATE DUE	

The Urbana Free Library
To renew: call 217-367-4057
or go to "*urbanafreelibrary.org*"
and select "Renew/Request Items"

NOT NEAR NORMAL
THE PARANORMAL

ALIENS
AND OTHER VISITORS

by Ruth Owen

Consultant: Karen Jaramillo
Library Manager
International UFO Museum and Research Center
Roswell, New Mexico

BEARPORT
PUBLISHING

New York, New York

Credits

Cover and Title Page, © Erlendur Konradsson/Shutterstock, © shiva3d/Shutterstock, and © Fer Gregory/Shutterstock; 5, © Andreas Meyer/Shutterstock and © iStockphoto/THinkstock; 6, © Chris Harvey/Shutterstock; 7, © iStockphoto/Thinkstock, © Alice Mary Herden Green-Fly Media LLC/Shutterstock, © sheelamohanachandran2010/Shutterstock, and © photobank.kiev.ua/Shutterstock; 8, © Albert Ziganshin/Shutterstock; 9, © YorkBerlin/Shutterstock; 10, © Andrea Danti/Shutterstock; 11, © Science Picture Co/Science Faction/Superstock; 12, © MarcelClemens/Shutterstock and © momopixs/Shutterstock; 12–13, © MaxFX/Shutterstock; 13, © Andreas Gradin/Shutterstock and © DarkGeometryStudios/Shutterstock; 15, © AF Archive/Alamy and © Fer Gregory/Shutterstock; 16–17, © rook76/Shutterstock and © Hemera/Thinkstock; 18–19, © Repina Valeriya/Shutterstock, © Christy Nicholas/Shutterstock, and © Linda Bucklin/Shutterstock; 20–21, © photobeard/Shutterstock; 22–23, © Manamana/Shutterstock; 23T, © The Ohio State University Radio Observatory and the North American AstroPhysical Observatory; 24–25, © diversepixel/Shutterstock and © Chris Harvey/Shutterstock; 27, 28L, 28R, 29T, © AF Archive/Alamy; 29B, © United Archives GmbH/Alamy.

Publisher: Kenn Goin
Editorial Director: Adam Siegel
Creative Director: Spencer Brinker
Design: Emma Randall
Editor: Mark J. Sachner
Photo Researcher: Ruby Tuesday Books Ltd

Library of Congress Cataloging-in-Publication Data in process at time of publication (2013)
Library of Congress Control Number: 2012045264
ISBN-13: 978-1-61772-723-8 (library binding)

For more information, write to Bearport Publishing Company, Inc., 45 West 21st Street, Suite 3B, New York, New York 10010. Printed in the United States of America.

10 9 8 7 6 5 4 3 2 1

Contents

Abducted!

On a winter night in 1995, eleven-year-old Jason Andrews woke up from a deep sleep. It was 3:00 A.M.—the time the visitors always came.

Suddenly, Jason saw a tall, thin creature rise up from the floor at the end of his bed. Then other, shorter creatures appeared in his bedroom. When the terrified boy tried to scream for help, no sound came out. Then, without knowing how he got there, Jason found himself in a cold, circular room that looked like it was in a hospital. When Jason looked up, he saw the tall creature **operating** on his stomach, but Jason felt no pain.

Then, in an instant, Jason was back at home, and it was morning. His ordeal was over, but Jason knew they would return again. Had Jason Andrews really been **abducted** by **aliens**?

The Alien Visitors

Jason described the aliens that abducted him as having thin, gray-colored bodies with large heads, huge black eyes, and tiny mouths and noses. The alien that Jason called "the tall one" was just over five feet (1.5 m) tall.

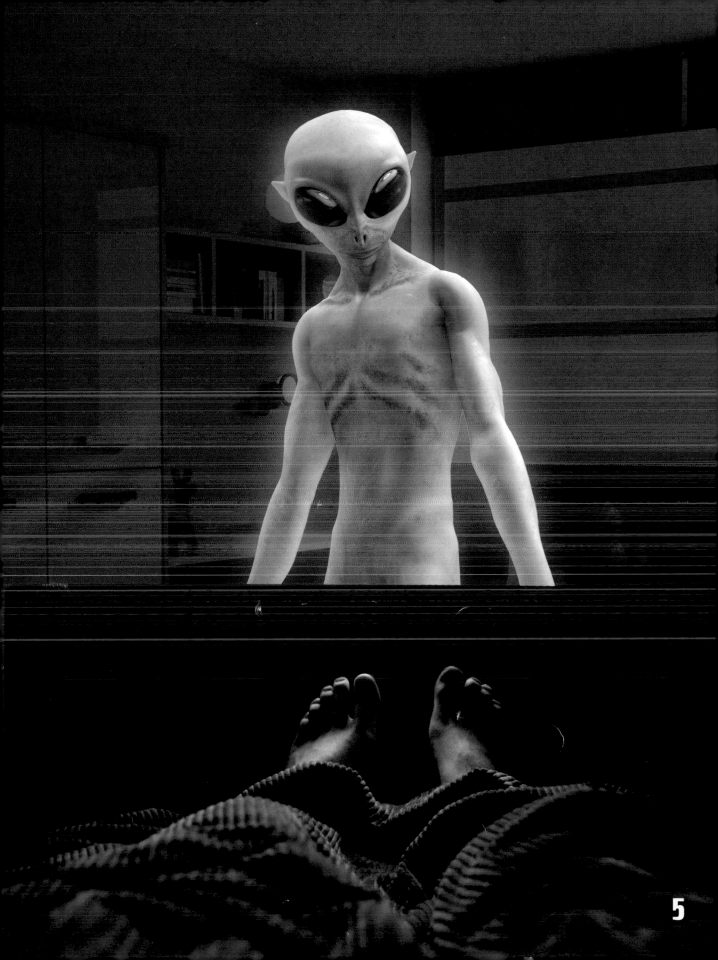

5

A Childhood of Terror

Jason Andrews believed he was an **abductee**—a person chosen by aliens to be carried off and studied. He was 12 years old before he finally told his parents about his alien encounters. The terrified boy explained that the creatures performed medical experiments on him.

Although his story was incredible, it helped explain many strange things that had happened to Jason over the years. As a little boy, Jason sometimes experienced terrible stomach pains. One time, a doctor discovered a long scar on Jason's side—and yet the boy had not been injured or even had an operation. A week later, the scar was gone, but new scars had mysteriously appeared on his stomach.

Was Jason Andrews really abducted by aliens? Were the scars on his body the work of an alien scientist? Only Jason will ever know the truth.

Baby Abductee

Jason told his parents that he remembered long, thin, gray fingers reaching into his crib and lifting him up when he was a toddler.

Alien Grays

Jason Andrews is one of thousands of people around the world who claim to have been abducted by aliens, or **extraterrestrials**. So what exactly are these terrifying creatures?

People who believe in aliens say they are intelligent creatures that come from planets far beyond our **solar system**. Like Jason, most abductees describe aliens as having thin, gray-colored bodies. These creatures, known as alien grays, are often described as having short legs and long arms with hands that reach down to their knees. Alien grays usually have three or four long fingers on each hand. Often, the fingers are webbed and have long fingernails or claws.

Alien grays are also said to have huge heads with large, **menacing** eyes and no hair on their heads or bodies. Some people who see the creatures describe them as wearing shiny, **metallic** space suits.

Alien grays

Reptilian alien

Reptilians

Some people say they have been abducted by large aliens that walk on two legs like humans but have scaly skin like **reptiles**. These creatures are known as reptilians.

Silent Screams

When people describe their abduction by alien grays, their memories are often very similar. The aliens usually appear in the person's bedroom. Then the aliens instantly **paralyze** their victim so that he or she can see and hear but cannot scream for help.

Most abductees say they are then taken to the aliens' spacecraft. Once inside, the aliens perform medical tests and examinations on the terrified, paralyzed abductees. Some victims feel no pain. Others endure hours of **agony**.

When the abduction is over, the person is usually returned home. Sometimes, the abductee feels as if only a few minutes have passed, but often several hours have gone by. Some abductees have no memory of what happened, while others remember every detail of their horrible ordeal.

They're Here

Some abductees say that bright lights shine into their bedroom windows when the aliens arrive. However, Jason Andrews always felt a strange tingling in his head when the extraterrestrials came to abduct him.

Extraterrestrial Scientists

If alien abduction stories are true, why would extraterrestrial creatures travel across the universe to kidnap humans? One theory is that the aliens are simply otherworldly scientists interested in studying other life-forms. Some abductees say their alien captors have inserted tiny **implants** into their heads. These people believe the implants allow the aliens to track their movements and study their behavior.

Some people also believe that aliens study Earth's animals. Jason Andrews is convinced that the aliens that attacked him also carried out experiments on his horse, as well as a cat, fox, and four mice. One night, Jason's horse had a large section of flesh cut from its shoulder. The severe wound didn't bleed, and the horse showed no sign of pain. The other animals were all found dead on the family's farm. Each one had a tiny, blood-free hole in its head.

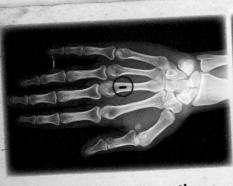
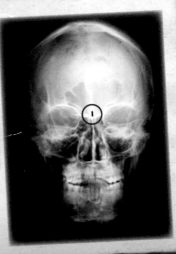

Some people believe these x-rays show alien implants inside human bodies.

Nordic Aliens

Some people claim to have met tall, muscular aliens known as Nordics. These aliens get their name because they have pale skin and white-blond hair, like people from northern Europe. Nordic aliens are usually reported as being gentle and friendly to humans.

Visitors in the Forest

One of the most famous alien abductions took place in Arizona in 1975. On a November evening, Travis Walton and six friends were riding home in their truck after a long day's work cutting trees in a forest.

Suddenly, the men saw a strange, yellow light shining from the sky. As they drove closer, they could see a large, saucer-shaped object hovering about 20 feet (6 m) above the ground.

The driver stopped the truck, and Travis climbed out to take a closer look. As his friends screamed not to get too close, Travis walked into the circle of yellow light below the **flying saucer**. Suddenly, a bolt of greenish-blue lightning blasted from the craft, knocking him to the ground. All Travis remembers feeling is a massive electric shock. Then everything went black.

Vanished

Travis's terrified friends sped away from the scene, leaving their friend behind. The men soon decided to go back to help Travis. However, when they returned, the forest was dark and quiet. There was no flying saucer and no Travis!

Alien Abductee

One moment, Travis Walton was in the forest with his friends. The next, he was lying on an examining table in a white room.

Suddenly, he saw a face with huge, shiny, dark eyes above him. In the room with Travis were three small, thin creatures with large, bald heads. Travis did not know where he was, but he felt sure he was aboard an alien spacecraft. When Travis struggled to his feet ready to fight his captors, they quietly left the room. On his own, Travis was then able to explore the spacecraft, until he suddenly woke up on the side of a highway.

After he awoke, Travis felt he had been gone for several hours. When he was reunited with his family and friends, however, he learned that he had been missing for five days! Travis Walton's story sounds unbelievable. To this day, however, Travis and his six friends say their incredible story of that November night is true.

Alien Captors

Travis described the aliens that abducted him as follows:

- Five feet (1.5 m) tall with a human-like shape
- Soft, white, marshmallow-like flesh
- No hair, eyelashes, or eyebrows
- Thin fingers with no fingernails
- Wearing one-piece orange suits

The Hopkinsville Encounter

Another terrifying alien attack occurred on an August night in 1955. That evening, Billy Ray Taylor was visiting the Sutton family at their farmhouse near Hopkinsville, Kentucky. At around 8:00 P.M., the Sutton's dog began barking loudly. Billy Ray and Elmer Sutton grabbed shotguns and went outside to investigate. To their shock, walking toward the house was a three-foot (1 m) tall, greenish-silver creature with big eyes and large, pointed ears. The men shot at the alien **intruder**, but the bullets had no effect.

The men rushed back inside, but the terror was just beginning. Over the next few hours, small alien faces peered in the windows and doors of the house. The creatures could also be heard climbing on the roof. Billy Ray and Elmer shot at the aliens again and again, but their weapons did no harm. Finally, Billy Ray and the Suttons ran to their cars and escaped.

Unable to Forget

To this day, everyone who witnessed the 1955 attack claims it really happened. Some of the victims were so terrified, they could hardly bring themselves to tell their stories.

Roswell

There are many stories of aliens and their spacecraft landing on Earth, but can anyone prove they exist? Some people believe the U.S. government has evidence.

In early July 1947, it is thought that a **UFO** crashed in the desert near Roswell, New Mexico. Investigators from the Roswell Army Air Field found a wide **gouge** in the desert. They determined that something had smashed into and then slid along the sandy ground for hundreds of feet. At the site, people also found thin pieces of a strange metal that seemed **indestructible**.

On July 8, the army reported that a flying saucer had crashed in the area. The next day, however, army officials changed their story, saying that the crashed UFO was actually a **weather balloon**. Many people believe that this was a big government cover-up. Did the army really find a crashed UFO near Roswell, and was the U.S. government trying to keep the discovery a secret?

Alien Bodies

Many people believe the army found alien bodies in the crashed UFO at Roswell. After the crash, an army officer called a local funeral home to inquire about getting several small coffins and to ask about how to **preserve** dead bodies.

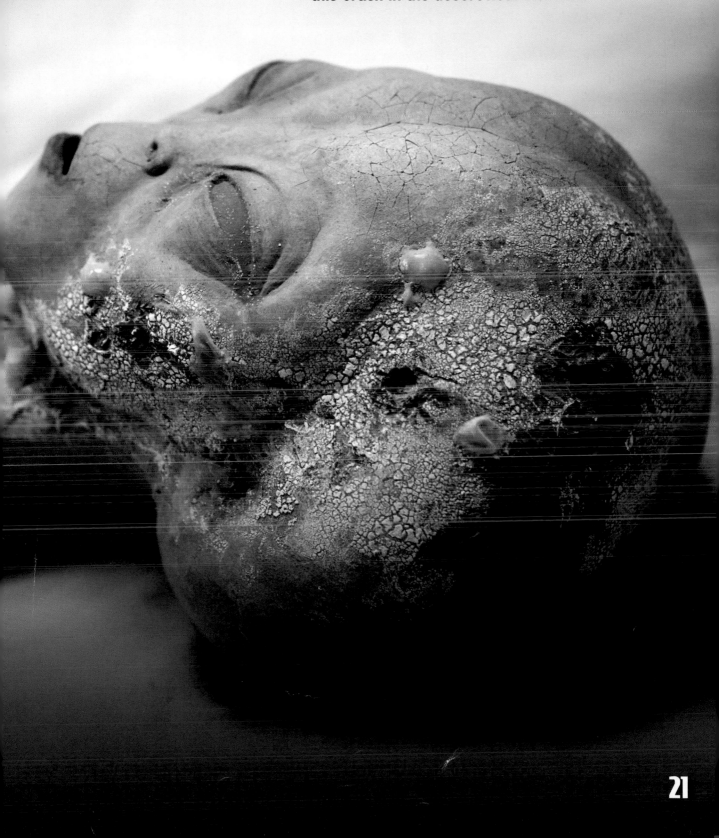

This is a model of a dead alien at the Roswell UFO Museum. Did creatures that looked like this crash in the desert near Roswell?

Searching for Alien Messages

Many scientists are looking for proof that human beings are not the only intelligent life-forms in the universe. Humans do not yet have the **technology** to build a spacecraft that could travel trillions of miles to search for alien neighbors. However, one way that scientists can look for other life-forms is to try to pick up messages or signals from other worlds.

The SETI (search for extraterrestrial intelligence) project brings together scientists from around the world who use powerful **radio telescopes** to scan the universe to pick up **radio waves**. The scientists then use computers to analyze the radio waves for special codes that could be a sign that an alien world exists.

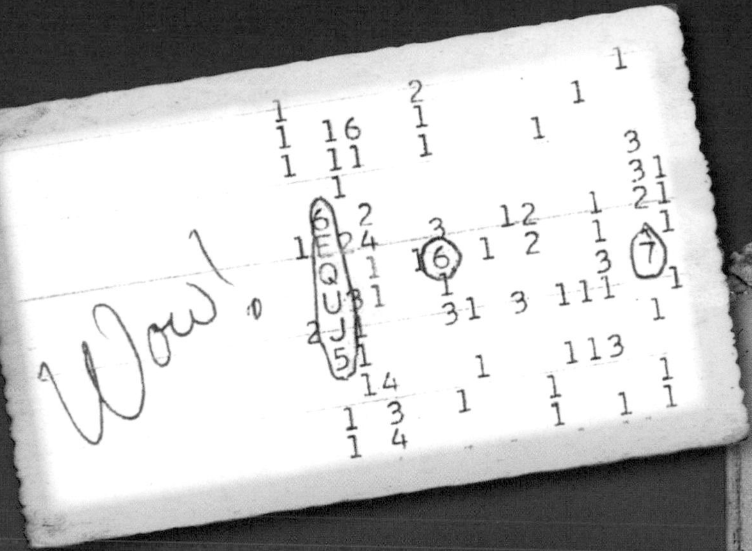

The "Wow!" Signal

In August 1977, scientist Jerry Ehman was studying radio waves from outer space. Suddenly, he saw a strange combination of letters and numbers showing an unusually strong signal. Even today, no one knows what this radio signal means. It is known as the "Wow!" signal, however, after Jerry's excited note in red ink.

Radio telescopes in New Mexico

Are We Alone?

Because the universe is so vast, many people think that Earth cannot possibly be the only planet where there are living things. So how many other planets are there in space?

In our **galaxy** alone, the Milky Way, there are around 400 billion stars, including the Sun. Many of these stars are likely to be surrounded by planets. The Milky Way is just one galaxy, though. In the entire universe, there may be 100 billion different galaxies. This all adds up to many trillions of planets and places that aliens might possibly call home. Who knows what alien **civilization** could be watching Earth at this very moment.

Alien Animals and Plants

Humans share Earth with hundreds of thousands of different animals, plants, and microscopic living things such as bacteria. Maybe aliens also share their home planets with thousands of alien animals, plants, and microorganisms!

Could distant planets be
home to vast alien cities?

25

Fact or Fiction?

Is it possible that there are aliens living somewhere in the universe that have traveled to Earth? Or are the thousands of alien abductees just telling lies? Some people believe that abductees may be making up stories or have unknowingly based their experiences on dreams—or nightmares.

The fact is that people who believe they have been abducted by aliens have little proof to back up their stories. Some claim this is because aliens are too intelligent to leave behind clues. They believe that aliens can paralyze any witnesses who might be nearby. Also, abductees say that aliens can stop electronic equipment such as video recorders from working during an abduction.

For now, no one knows for sure if aliens exist and whether the abduction stories are true. Could aliens visit your neighborhood tonight? Maybe they will abduct one of your neighbors or a family member—they might even choose you!

Are You an Abductee?

Not everyone remembers being abducted. This useful list will help you watch for signs that aliens are visiting you.

- Do you often see strange lights in the sky?
- Do you sometimes wake up somewhere other than your bedroom?
- Do strange marks appear on your body overnight?
- Do you get nosebleeds? If your answer is yes, you may have an alien implant in your head that was inserted through your nose.

An alien creature from the movie *Aliens vs. Predator: Requiem*

Aliens in the Movies

Many movies have featured extraterrestrials. Here are a few examples of the most famous aliens that have appeared on the big screen.

E.T. the Extra-Terrestrial

Description and behavior: E.T. is a gentle, curious, child-sized alien with brown, wrinkled skin. He has a large head and a long neck and arms.

Making contact: E.T. comes to Earth with other extraterrestrials to study plants and is accidentally left behind by his spaceship. E.T. is then discovered by a young boy named Elliot, and the two become friends.

Alien abilities: E.T. can bring dead plants back to life by touching them with his glowing finger. He also learns to speak English in just a few hours by listening to humans and watching TV.

Independence Day

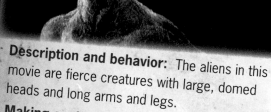

Description and behavior: The aliens in this movie are fierce creatures with large, domed heads and long arms and legs.

Making contact: The aliens travel to Earth in a huge mother ship that carries 36 smaller spacecraft within it. The aliens then use the small flying saucers to destroy major cities around the world and kill thousands of people.

Alien abilities: The aliens are able to enter and control the minds of humans. The aliens also use deadly weapons in an attempt to kill all life-forms on Earth.

Avatar

Description and behavior: The Na'vi aliens live on Pandora, a forest-covered moon that is trillions of miles from Earth. The Na'vi are blue, human-like creatures. They are about 12 feet (3.6 m) tall and have long tails.

Making contact: Humans invade Pandora to search for and steal a metal that is needed on Earth. The humans begin to destroy Pandora, which forces the peaceful Na'vi to fight back to protect their world

Alien abilities: Na'vi are able to communicate with trees and bond with Pandora's wild creatures. The Na'vi tame wild, flying, dragon-like animals and ride on their backs.

Close Encounters of the Third Kind

Description and behavior: The aliens are peaceful, child-sized alien grays that have no hair and wear no clothes.

Making contact: The alien grays first visit Earth in small UFOs. Then the aliens' giant mother ship lands in Wyoming. From there, more aliens emerge alongside many human abductees.

Alien abilities: The alien grays send a message to Earth using a musical tune. The message tells human scientists where to meet the aliens when they land on Earth.

Glossary

abducted (ab-DUK-tid) taken away against one's will, or kidnapped

abductee (ab-duk-TEE) someone who has been taken away against his or her will, or kidnapped

agony (AG-uh-nee) extreme suffering

aliens (AY-lee-uhnz) creatures from outer space

civilization (*siv*-uh-li-ZAY-shuhn) a large group of people (or alien beings, if from another world) sharing a common location, culture, way of life, and set of values

extraterrestrials (*ek*-struh-tuh-RESS-tree-uhlz) beings from other planets

flying saucer (FLYE-ing SAW-sur) a type of UFO that looks like a big disk

galaxy (GAL-uhk-see) a large group of stars

gouge (GOUJ) a large hole or indentation in a surface

implants (IM-plantss) objects inserted into something else, such as a living body, usually by surgery

indestructible (in-di-STRUK-tuh-buhl) unbreakable, not able to be destroyed

intruder (in-TROOD-ur) someone who enters a place without permission

menacing (MEN-iss-ing) frightening or threatening

metallic (meh-TAL-ik) made of or looking like metal

operating (OP-uh-rate-ing) performing surgery

paralyze (PA-ruh-lize) to cause something or someone to be unable to move

preserve (pri-ZURV) to treat something with chemicals so that it doesn't rot

radio telescopes (RAY-dee-oh TEL-uh-skohpss) instruments used to detect radio waves or radiation and their sources

radio waves (RAY-dee-oh WAYVZ) signals that carry, or transmit, electricity; are often used to send words or images over vast distances

reptiles (REP-tilez) cold-blooded animals that usually have dry, scaly skin

solar system (SOH-lur SISS-tuhm) a star and all the planets, moons, meteors, and other objects that travel around it

technology (tek-NOL-uh-jee) the use of science to do practical or useful things

UFO (YOO EF OH) (Unidentified Flying Object) an object seen in the air that cannot be explained by human activities or nature

weather balloon (WETH-ur buh-LOON) a balloon that is sent into the atmosphere with instruments that measure weather conditions

Bibliography

Andrews, Ann, and Jean Ritchie. *Abducted: The True Tale of Alien Abduction in Rural England.* London: Headline (1998).

Roswell UFO Museum: www.roswellufomuseum.com

The Official Site of Travis Walton: www.travis-walton.com

Read More

Grey, Allen. *Alienology: The Complete Book of Extraterrestrials (Ologies).* Somerville, MA: Candlewick (2010).

Pipe, Jim. *Aliens (Tales of Horror).* New York: Bearport (2007).

Rooney, Anne. *Alien Abduction (Crabtree Contact).* New York: Crabtree (2008).

Learn More Online

To learn more about aliens, visit
www.bearportpublishing.com/NotNearNormal

Index

About the Author

Ruth Owen has been developing, editing, and writing children's books for more than ten years. She lives in Cornwall, England, just minutes from the ocean. Ruth loves gardening and caring for her family of llamas.